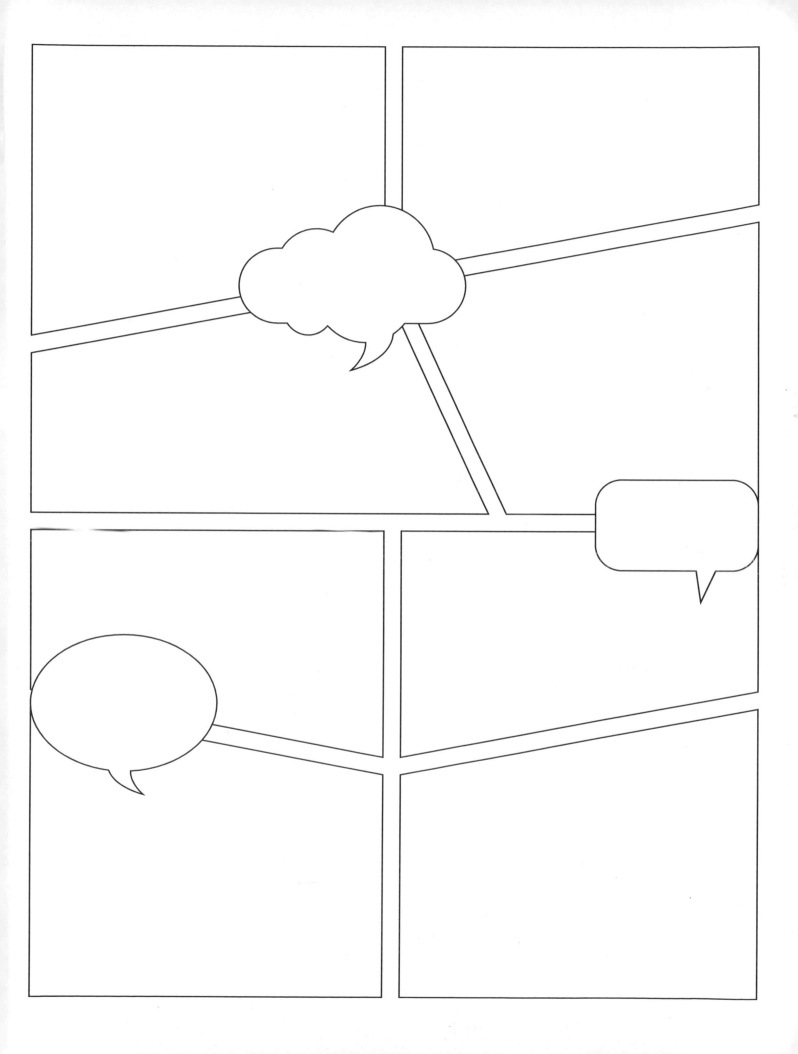

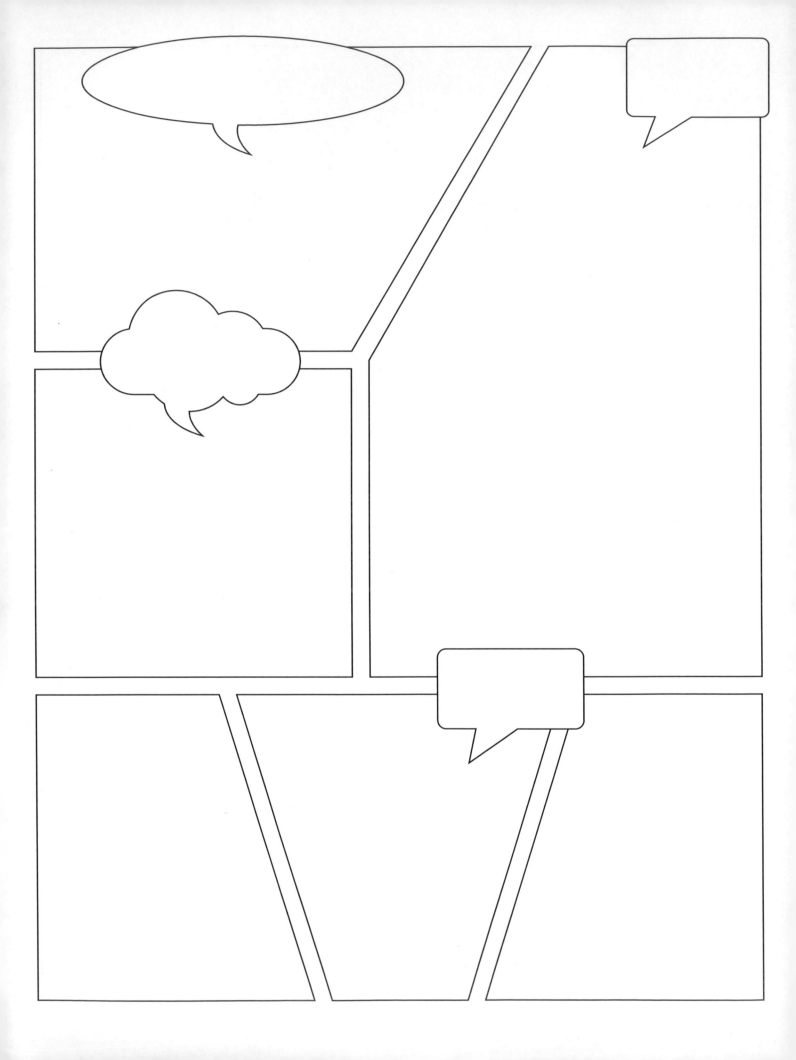

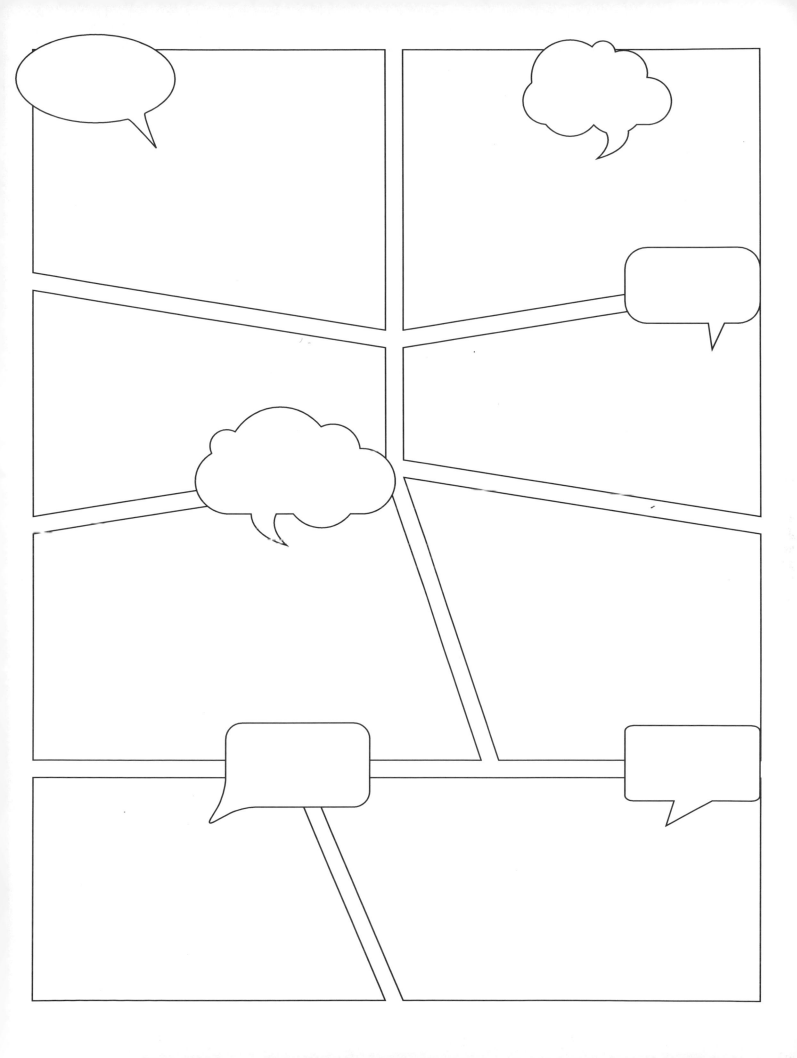

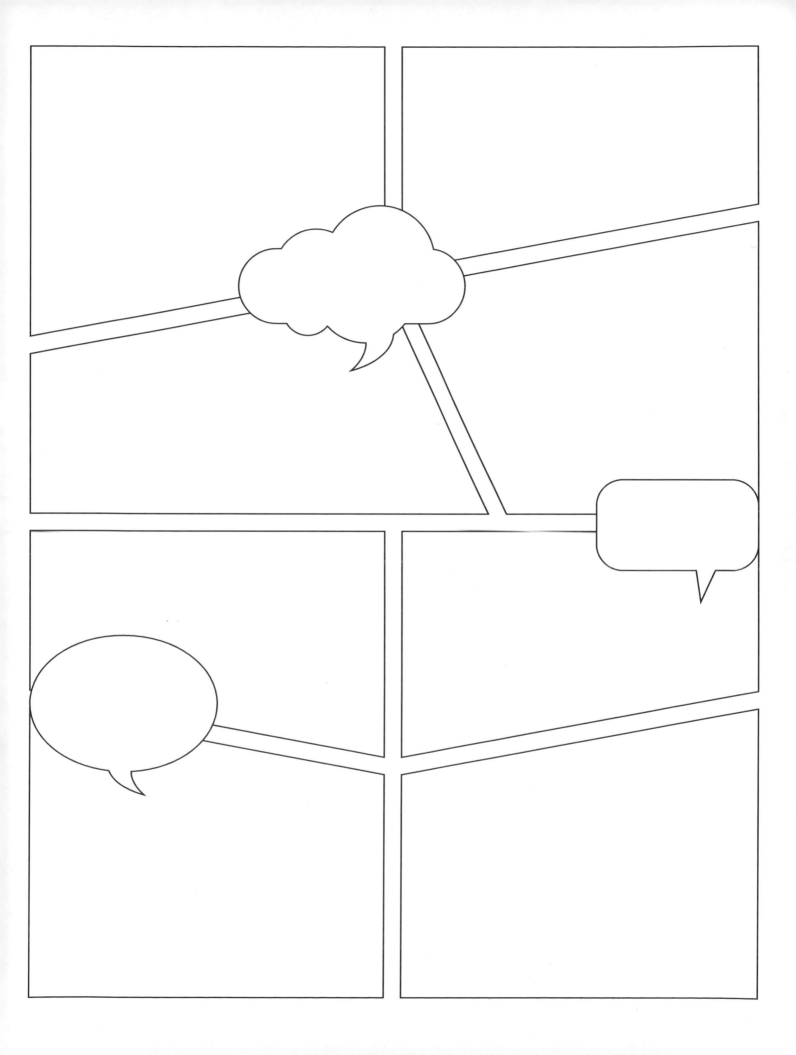

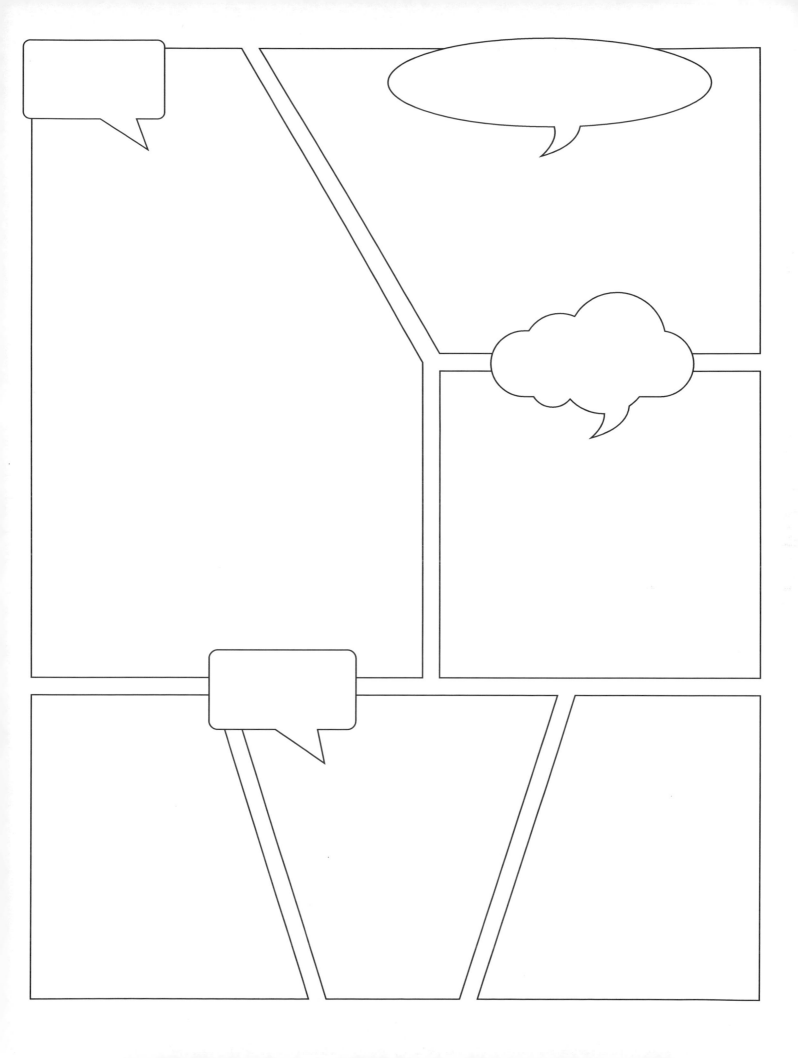

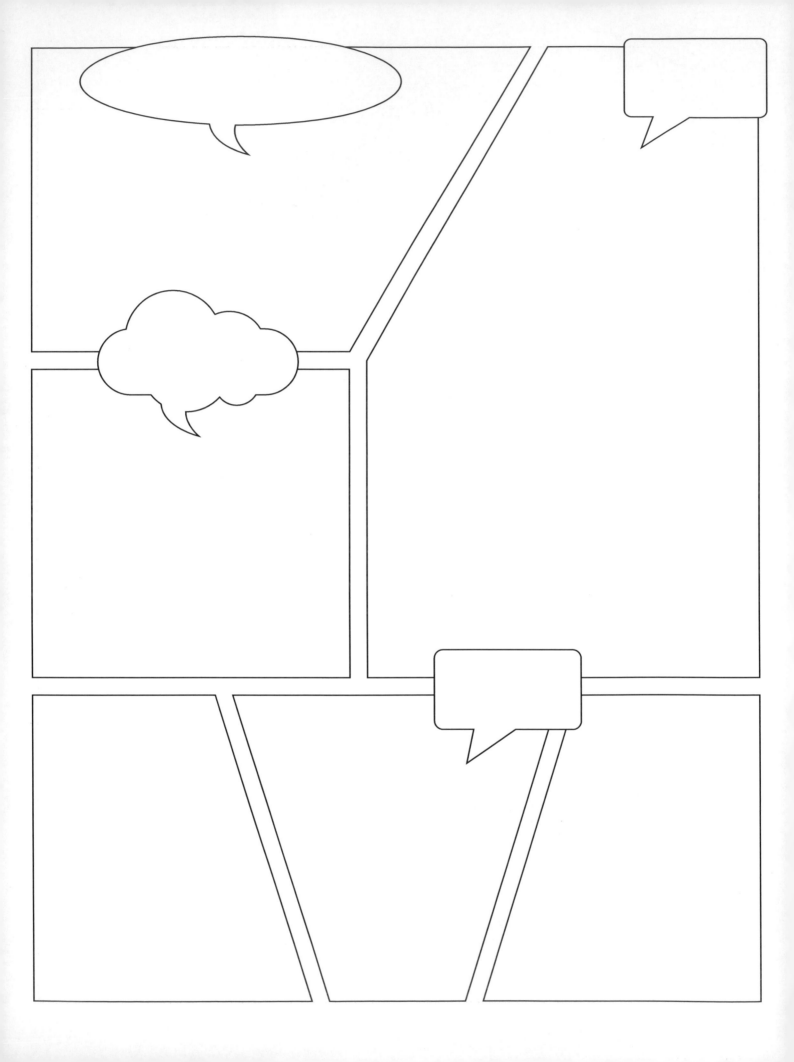

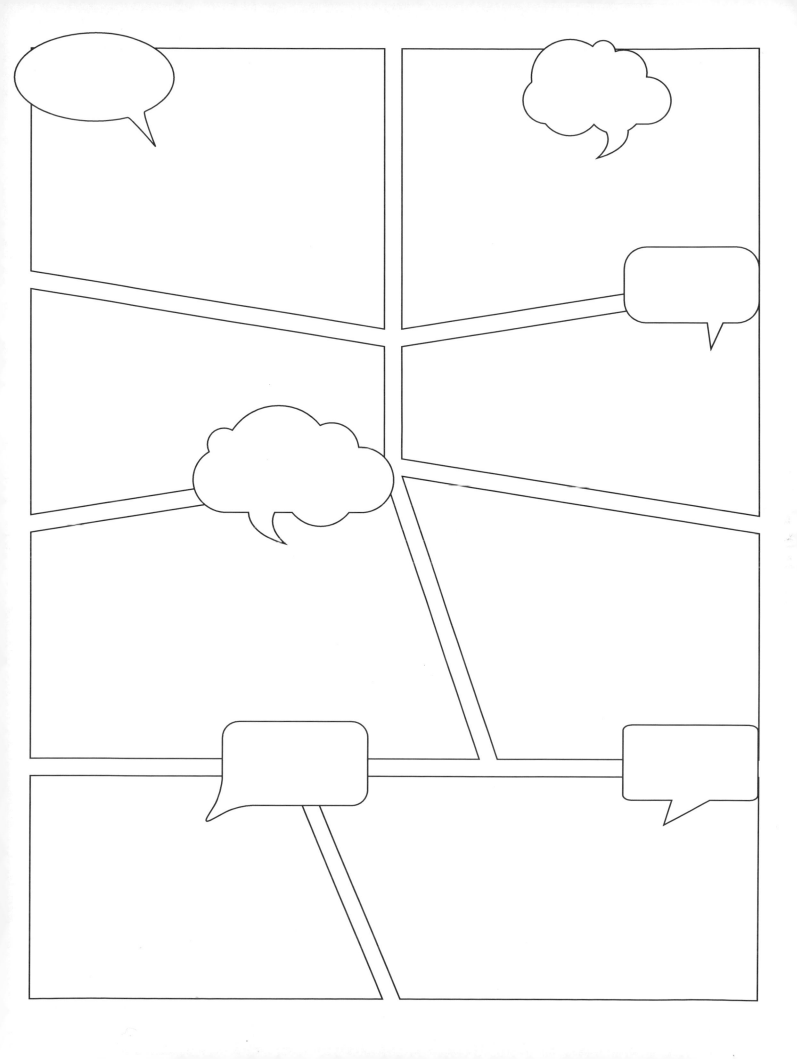

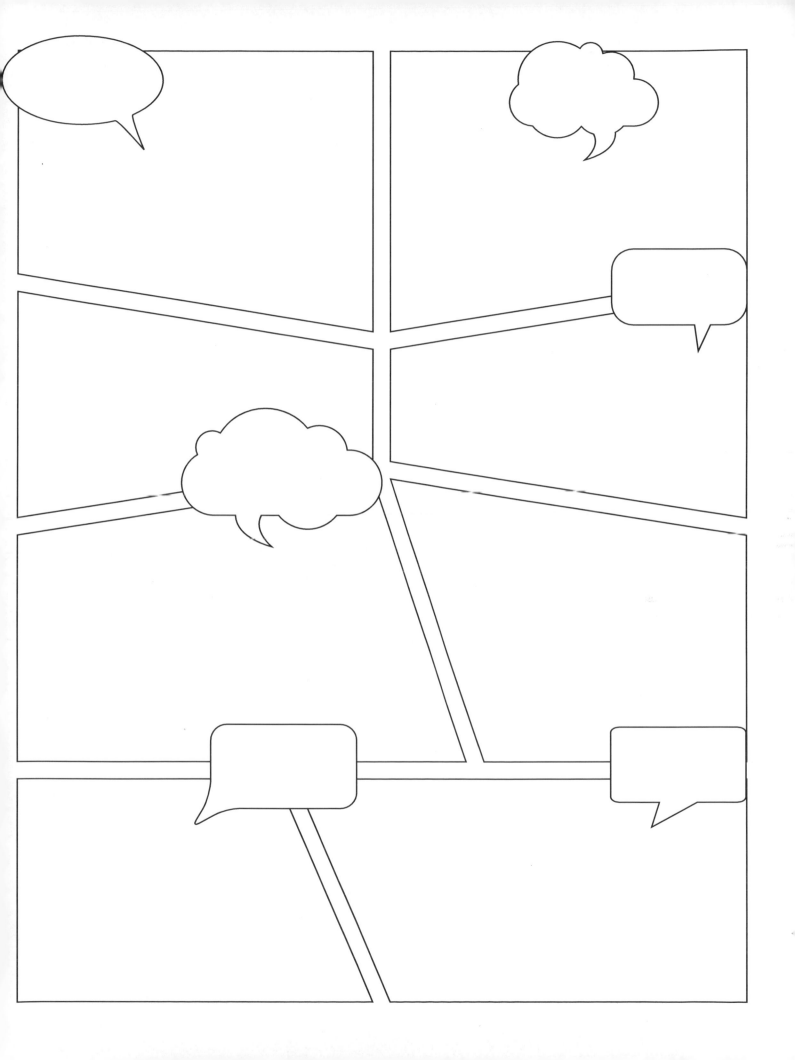

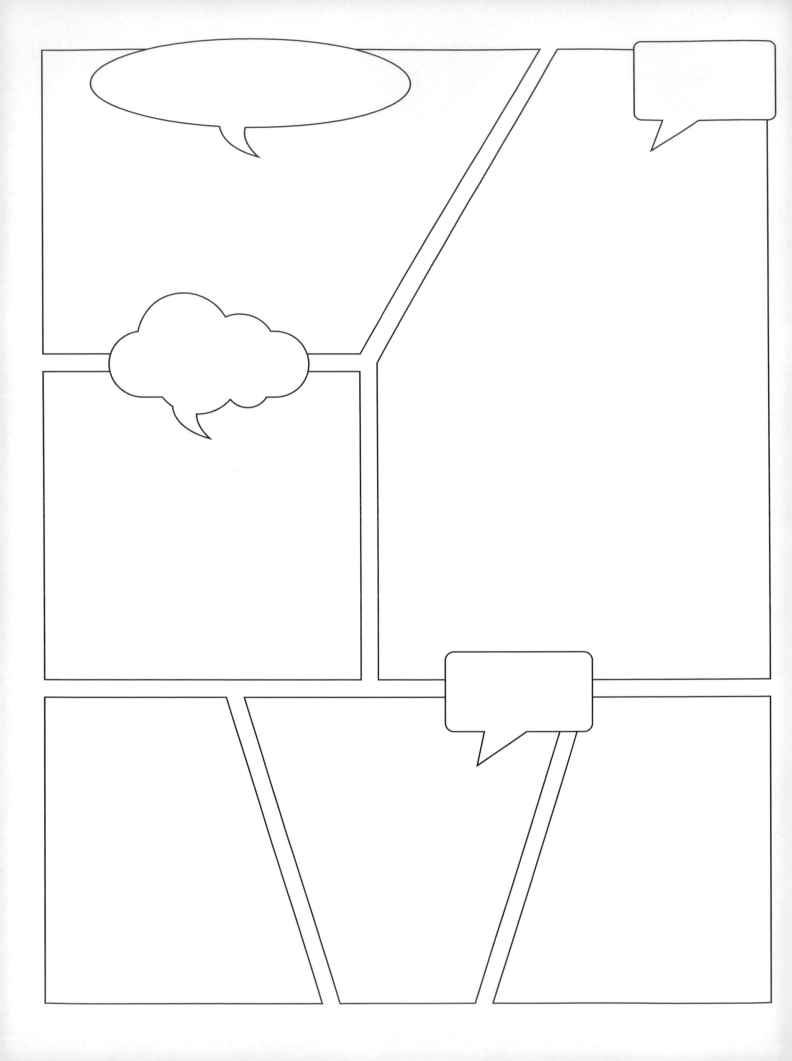

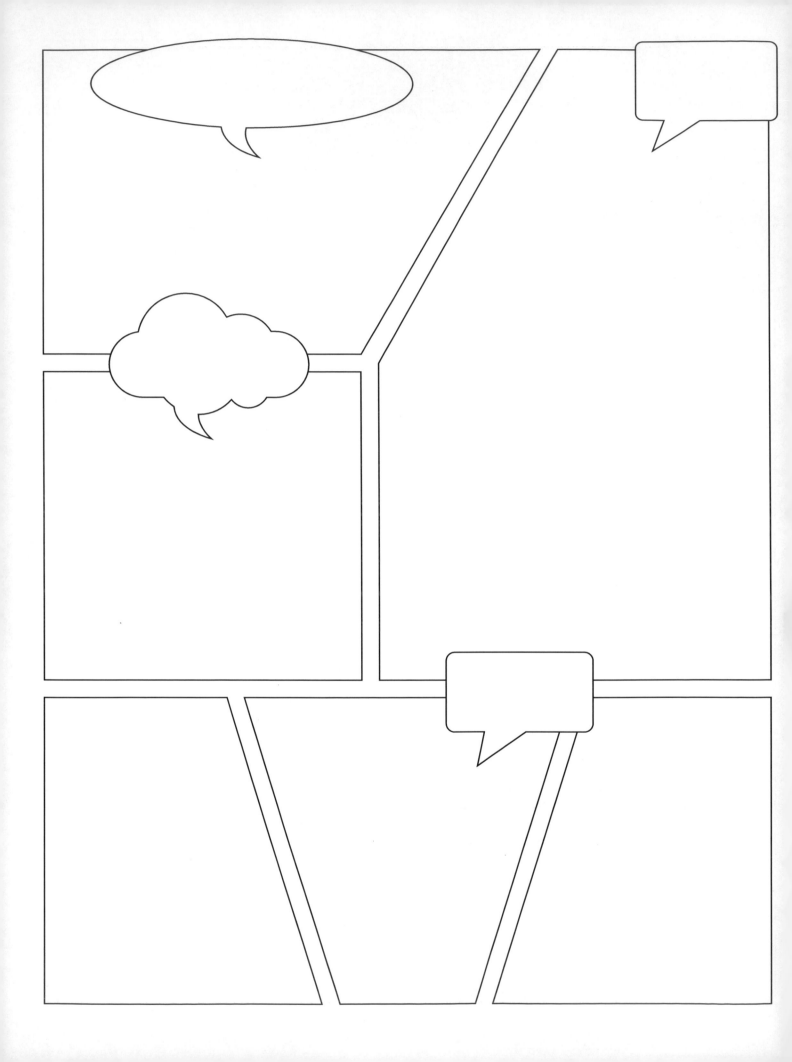

Printed in Great Britain
by Amazon

Want free goodies?
Email us at freebies@pbleu.com

 @PapeterieBleu

 @Papeterie Bleu

Shop our other books at
www.pbleu.com

Wholesale distribution through Ingram Content Group
www.ingramcontent.com/publishers/distribution/wholesale

For questions and customer service, email us at
support@pbleu.com